The Debate About
Euthanasia

KAYE STEARMAN

Published in 2011 by The Rosen Publishing Group Inc.
29 East 21st Street, New York, NY 10010

First Edition

Commissioning Editor: Jennifer Sanderson
Designer: Rita Storey
Picture Researcher: Kathy Lockley
Proofreader: Susie Brooks

Library of Congress Cataloging-in-Publication Data

Stearman, Kaye.
  The debate about euthanasia / Kaye Stearman. — 1st ed.
    p. cm. — (Ethical debates)
  Includes bibliographical references (p.   ) and index.
  ISBN 978-1-4358-9652-9 (library binding)
  ISBN 978-1-4358-9658-1 (paperback)
  ISBN 978-1-4358-9661-1 (6-pack)
  1. Euthanasia—Moral and ethical aspects—Juvenile literature. I. Title.
  R726.S673 2011
  179.7—dc22
                             2009050724

Photo Credits:
The author and publisher would like to thank the following agencies for allowing these pictures to be
reproduced: Action Press/Rex Features: title page, 22; AKG Images: 33; Bryan & Cherry Alexander/Alamy:
10; Vince Bevan/Alamy: 8; Leland Bobbé/Corbis: 26; Richard Crampton/Rex Features: 37; DD/Keystone
USA/Rex Features: 21; East News, Poland: 43; ER productions Ltd/Getty Images: 6; Fancy/Veer/Corbis: 13,
14, 17; Getty Images: 7, 25; Sally & Richard Greenhill/Alamy: 28; David A. Harvey/Getty Images: 18;
imagebroker/Alamy: 9; Frantzesco Kangaris/ Newsquest(SL): 35; Moodboard/Alamy: 34; PA/PA Archive/PA
Photos: 31; PHOTOTAKE Inc/Alamy: 45; Reuters/Corbis: 44; Patrick Robert/Sygma/Corbis: 20; John
Robertson/Alamy: 15; Norbert Schaefer/Corbis: 27; Handout Courtesy of the Schiavo Family/Corbis: 5;
Sipa Press/Rex Features: 40; Trevor Smith/Alamy: 36; Sean Sprague/Alamy: 29; Liss Steve/Corbis Sygma:
41; Ray Tang/Rex Features: 39; United States Holocaust Memorial Museum: 32; Voisin/Phanie/Rex
Features: Cover, 16. Every attempt has been made to clear copyright. Should there be any inadvertent
omission please apply to the publisher for rectification.

Manufactured in China
CPSIA Compliance Information: Batch #WAS0102YA: For Further Information
Contact Rosen Publishing, New York, New York at 1-800-237-9932

contents

Real-Life Case Study

This real-life case study highlights some of the issues that surround the debate on euthanasia.

case study

Terri Schiavo

Terri Schiavo was 41 when she died in Florida. For 15 years, she had been kept alive by artificial means. When she died, it was the result of a deliberate act in which her life support was withdrawn by doctors. It was not a quiet or easy death, nor was it a private one. The decision to allow her to die was fought through the U.S. courts, in the media, and on the streets by pro- and anti-euthanasia demonstrators. What started as a private tragedy spiraled into a public debate about euthanasia.

In 1990, without warning, Terri had stopped breathing and suffered a massive heart attack. Attempts were made to resuscitate her, but her brain had been deprived of oxygen for too long. When she emerged from a two-month coma, she went into a "sleep-wake cycle." She did not appear to be aware of herself, others, or her environment, nor did she respond to stimuli. Terri was fed through a tube into her stomach. Over the following years, a series of doctors identified her as being in a "persistent vegetative state" (PVS)—described as "wakefulness without awareness."

Doctors said that it was extremely unlikely that she would ever recover but her family spent years in hope, trying different therapies without success. In 1998, her husband, Michael, petitioned the Florida courts that the hospital be allowed to remove her feeding tube so that she could die. Among other things, the court considered what Terri's wishes would have been had she been in a position to decide. She had not made a "living will" (a legal document that outlines wishes if a patient becomes terminally ill or permanently incapacitated), but the court heard that she had expressed a wish not to "be kept alive on a machine." Her parents opposed the petition saying that she was a devout Catholic and so could not consent to euthanasia.

The initial court hearing set the stage for an epic legal battle between lawyers representing Michael Schiavo on one side and her parents on the other. The case went through to the Supreme Court and there were attempts at legislation in Florida and Washington, D.C. The case was personally acrimonious, with Terri's parents accusing Michael of exploitation and abuse. The case was highly controversial and attracted attention in the media and from religious and political figures, including President George W. Bush. There were demonstrations before the courts and before the hospice where Terri stayed. Twice, Terri's feeding tube was withdrawn, then reinstated by court order.

The final court ruling was that Terri could be allowed to die. On March 18, 2005, her feeding tube was removed. She died 14 days later. Years later, the controversy remains.

viewpoints

"I'm absolutely in agreement with the argument that if pain is insufferable, then someone should be given help to die, but I feel there's a wider argument that if somebody absolutely, desperately wants to die because they're a burden to their family, or the state, then I think they, too, should be allowed to die."

Baroness Mary Warnock, philosopher and medical ethicist, September 2004

"We know that some of the most distressing situations arise from individuals' anxiety about maintaining their dignity at the end of life, combined with concern about the availability of effective palliative care. We believe that with proper pain control, good communication, and psychological support, far fewer people would consider asking for clinical help to die."

Statement from the British Medical Association and the Royal College of Nursing, December 2004

It's a Fact

Medical research has documented that there is no chance of recovery for a person who has been in a persistent vegetative state (PVS) for 12 months or more. PVS is different from a coma, in which a person has his or her eyes closed and lacks sleep-wake cycles, and from the "locked-in" syndrome, where sufferers are aware of themselves and their environment, but have lost movement and speech, communicating through eye movement or blinks.

▼ Terri Schiavo, shown here with her mother, became the center of a highly controversial court case fought between her husband and her parents. Although she appears responsive in this photo, she was in a persistent vegetative state and unaware of herself or her environment.

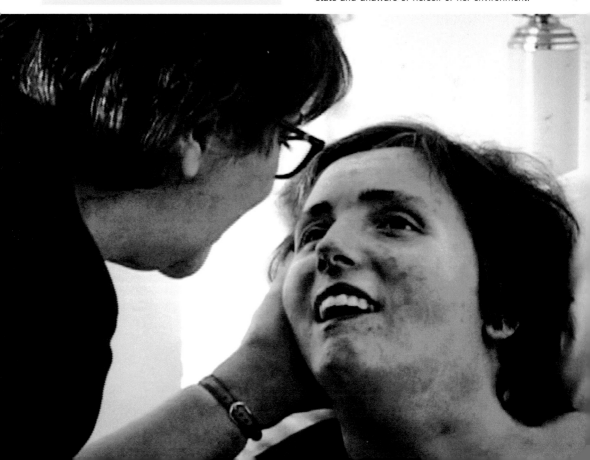

CHAPTER 1

What Is Euthanasia?

Euthanasia is literally a matter of life and death. Although it is still a relatively rare occurrence, it is an issue that is highly controversial and is regularly debated in the media. The word "euthanasia" is derived from ancient Greek and can be translated as "good death." Today, it refers to the deliberate killing of a person, by oneself or by others. It normally applies when the person is close to death, or in extreme and untreatable pain, or is kept alive by artificial means without hope of recovery.

Voluntary or Involuntary Euthanasia

Euthanasia is generally classified as voluntary and involuntary. Voluntary euthanasia, also called euthanasia by consent, is where the affected person makes their own decision to die. The person may act alone if he or she is physically capable, but in many cases, people do not have the ability to do so (usually through sickness, pain, or disability), and so ask others to assist them. This is often referred to as "assisted dying" or "assisted suicide." If a doctor assists, then it is called "physician-assisted suicide."

▼ A doctor performs cardiopulmonary resuscitation (CPR) on a patient in a hospital emergency room. Advances in emergency medicine have resulted in many more lives being saved.

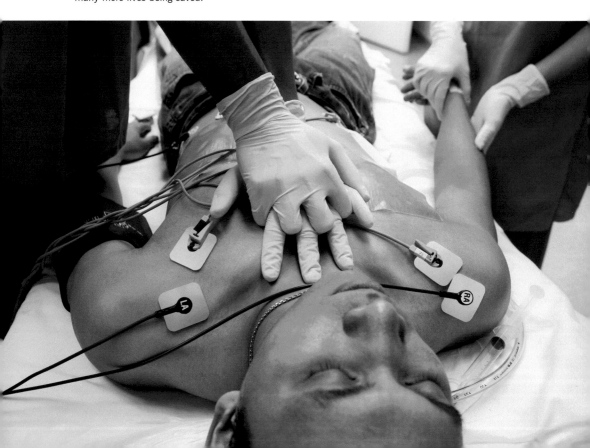

Involuntary euthanasia is where another person, usually a family member, makes the decision to enable the affected person to die because he or she is incapable of making this decision personally. This may be acting on the spoken or written wishes of the person before he or she becomes incapacitated, or on the basis of religious or ethical beliefs. In some cases, the decision may be taken on "quality of life" grounds—in other words, looking at the pain and suffering of the person and whether he or she is likely to recover. This is one of the most controversial forms of euthanasia.

Means of Euthanasia

Euthanasia can also be divided into different categories to denote the means used to cause death. Passive euthanasia entails the withholding of established treatments (such as surgery or medicines) or medication that relieves pain (such as morphine) but might also cause death. This practice is most often applied in a hospital or hospice with a patient who is frail, in pain, or close to death, and in agreement with the patient or his or her family members.

Nonaggressive euthanasia is the withdrawal of life-support equipment, such as a feeding tube or breathing apparatus. Aggressive euthanasia is where there is a definite act to cause death, usually through the use of lethal substances, such as poisons or drugs. Sometimes, sufferers take the final step themselves, but if they are not able to do this, they can be partially or wholly assisted by another person.

▲ Noel Martin was paralyzed from the neck down after an unprovoked racial attack in Germany in 1996. Despite his disability, he campaigned against racism in Britain and Germany. In 2006, he announced that he would choose to die with the Swiss euthanasia organization, Dignitas, on July 23, 2007 (his 48th birthday), but later, he postponed his death.

It's a Fact

Modern China's first known euthanasia case occurred in 1986 when Mr. Wang Ming-Cheng asked Dr. Pu Liansheng to help his sick, elderly mother to die. In 1992, a court judged both not guilty of murder.

Is It Murder?

Although many opponents of euthanasia see it as murder, euthanasia has a different moral basis to murder. Like euthanasia, murder is a deliberate killing, but it is always involuntary and done out of greed, anger, revenge, or other selfish reasons.

Opponents say that euthanasia is a disguised form of murder with similar motives. For example, a sick or disabled person may be pressured to ask doctors not to be treated with expensive drugs or surgery in order to relieve his or her family from financial stress or to save a dwindling inheritance. Supporters of euthanasia reply that most families want to see their relative live, whatever the cost, and often, it is the affected person who makes the decision to die in opposition to their family's wishes.

The most controversial form of euthanasia is aggressive euthanasia, where people make a decision to die, by their own hand or with the assistance of others. Most of these people have a terminal illness or are in pain. Supporters point out that often they make their decision several years before they expect to die, knowing that their condition will worsen, and they may not be in a position to make a rational decision later on. But opponents point out that people in this situation can still be manipulated or make an irrational decision.

There is also controversy about the people who assist in acts of euthanasia. What are their motives for participating? Opponents say that although some may sincerely believe that they are helping a person they care about to escape an intolerable situation, others enjoy the attention or even get a vicarious thrill from being so close to death. Many supporters of euthanasia agree that some assistants may have dubious motives but say that this is because of the conditions in which euthanasia takes place—often in an illegal and hidden way.

Sometimes, a death may be classed as a "mercy killing," although this is not a legal category. Mercy killings usually involve a family member causing or hastening the death of a sick or disabled person out of grief or despair. Often the person gives himself or herself up to the authorities and pleads guilty. In many countries, such cases are treated leniently, and given little or a symbolic punishment, such as a suspended jail sentence.

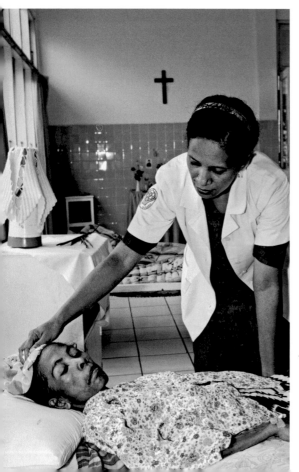

◄ A doctor tends a patient with tuberculosis in a hospital in East Timor. As in many poorer countries, facilities are limited and treatment is limited to the most common diseases.

These mercy killings are sometimes thought of as a form of involuntary euthanasia. Mercy killings can have a devastating effect on those involved. Figures from Britain show that 30 percent of family members involved in mercy killings go on to commit suicide themselves.

Suicide

Many people consider euthanasia to be suicide, or self-killing, which is not only illegal in many countries but also forbidden by many religious teachings. Supporters point out that although suicide can be performed for various reasons, for example, because a person is depressed, confused, or under the influence of alcohol or drugs, euthanasia is not suicide in the normal sense of the word, because it is mainly deliberate or premeditated. Opponents cannot see any difference and say that many so-called cases of euthanasia are people who have killed themselves out of confusion or despair rather than as a rational choice. For this reason, most countries with laws allowing euthanasia insist that people wishing to die through euthanasia must first undertake psychological testing to ensure that they are not disturbed or depressed and that their decision is a rational one.

Euthanasia in History

Euthanasia is not a common practice. This may be because until recently, most people lived relatively short lives. Infant mortality was high and only a minority of people lived into old age. If people had a serious illness or injury, they were much more likely to die than they would be today because of the limitations of medical care. However, there are some accounts of euthanasia being used in different societies throughout history.

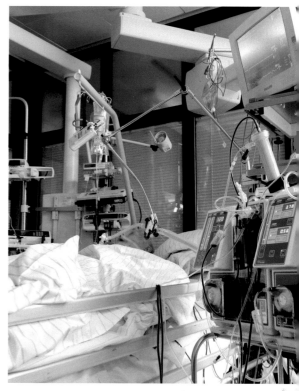

▲ A patient has kidney dialysis in Germany. Similar high-tech medical treatment is routinely available in affluent countries to reduce people's suffering.

Some forms of euthanasia were practiced in ancient Greece. The Spartans were a war-loving people who wanted to ensure that their future warriors would grow into healthy and hardy children. Therefore, newborn babies were exposed on a mountainside. Only the toughest survived and there were no attempts to save the weakest babies. Other groups also allowed babies who had physical defects to die. In the third century B.C.E., men of the island of Kea could end their life with the agreement of their fellow citizens. They would drink the poison hemlock and die amid rejoicing from the crowds. In both Greek and Roman society, there were other cases of assisted suicide—sometimes to avoid public disgrace or military defeat.

The Growth of New Religions

The religious beliefs of the ancient world saw death as a gift from the gods and not necessarily as something to be feared or avoided. The growth of the Christian Church saw a change in public attitudes, reflecting the new religious beliefs. Like Judaism before it, and Islam that followed it, Christianity supported a different view of death. Life itself was sacred. Death was an act to be decided by God, and suicide was a sin that could lead to damnation of the immortal soul. Supporting a person to die was also a sin and was condemned by the Church.

Although Judaism, Christianity, and Islam have evolved and changed over the centuries, the belief in the wrongness of suicide and euthanasia remains. However, in recent times, some religious groups have offered support for circumstances that could be termed passive euthanasia. For instance, the Catholic Church allows a terminal patient to refuse treatment that is regarded as "extraordinary" or "disproportionate," which is likely to cause more pain and suffering. However, the Catholic Church does not support any treatment that will hasten death.

The Inuit Peoples

Anthropologists have recorded accounts of euthanasia being practiced by some indigenous peoples, usually involving older people who can no longer hunt or move with the tribe. For example, among the Inuit peoples of the Arctic Circle, an elderly or sick person would sometimes walk into the icy wilderness to die of hunger and exposure, to avoid being a burden to the people. Today, this form of euthanasia is no longer practiced—the Inuit are mainly Christians and older people are supported by pensions and healthcare.

◀ An Inuit hunter from eastern Greenland sets a seal net under the sea ice to trap the seals that are part of the traditional Inuit diet. Like the Inuit of Canada and Alaska, their way of life has changed dramatically in the past century.

case study

Arrak Qulitalik

Arrak Qulitalik (also written as Aleak Kolitalik) was the respected leader of an Inuit community in the remote eastern Arctic settlement of Igloolik on the Melville Peninsula. Qulitalik was an old man when he died in 1963. He had already lived through an era of huge change for his people. In his youth, he had met the white explorers who were then claiming the northern lands as Canadian territory. He had lived and hunted across the north, using his skills to survive in the hostile lands. By the time of his death, most Inuit people were living in government settlements.

Qulitalik asked to die after contracting measles, a dangerous disease for which the Inuit people had no vaccine. He felt that his life was over. He asked three young men, Amak, Avinga, and Nangmalik, to help him to die. He told them that if they refused, after his death, his spirit would return and there would be no more seals or caribou for food. All three men played a part. One got the rifle, one the bullet, and one cocked the rifle. The whole community stood outside as Qulitalik shot himself four times, eventually dying the next day from shock and bleeding. None of the bullets had been fatal. The three young men buried the body and later wrote to the Catholic priest to explain their actions.

Amak, Avinga, and Nangmalik were arrested and became the first people to be tried under Canadian law for assisting a person to commit suicide. All three pleaded guilty. They said that they did not want to do it, but that they had to obey Arrak Qulitalik's wishes. Assisted suicide was part of Inuit tradition but they believed that what they had done was wrong. Although they were found guilty, the judge suspended their sentences and allowed them to return to their community.

viewpoints

"Just as I shall select my ship when I am about to go on a voyage, or my house when I propose to take a residence, so I shall choose my death when I am about to depart from life."

Seneca, Roman philosopher, Epistulae ad Lucilium, First century B.C.E.

"It is necessary to state firmly once more that nothing and no one can in any way permit the killing of an innocent human being, whether a fetus or an embryo, an infant or an adult, an old person, or one suffering from an incurable disease, or a person who is dying. Furthermore, no one is permitted to ask for this act of killing, either for himself or herself or for another person entrusted to his or her care, nor can he or she consent to it, either explicitly or implicitly, nor can any authority legitimately recommend or permit such an action."

Pope John Paul II, Declaration on Euthanasia, 1980

summary

▶ Euthanasia is the deliberate killing of a person by himself or herself or others, for the benefit of that person. There are significant differences between euthanasia, murder, and suicide.

▶ Euthanasia is usually divided into voluntary and involuntary euthanasia and into passive euthanasia, nonaggressive euthanasia, and aggressive euthanasia.

▶ Euthanasia has been used in particular circumstances by societies throughout history.

▶ Most religions are opposed to euthanasia.

CHAPTER 2

The Doctor's Dilemma

Medical ethics are the principles that govern the way doctors and other medical professionals conduct their work and their relationships with their patients. There is no one body of medical ethics used worldwide, although standard training programs and working practices have helped to bring different ethical frameworks closer together.

Most principles of medical ethics include:
- *Beneficence*—a doctor should always do the best for each patient, balancing the risks of different types of treatment against the likely benefits.
- *Nonmaleficence*—"do no harm"; a treatment should not worsen the patient's health or well-being.
- *Truthfulness*—a patient should be fully informed of his or her condition and the advantages and drawbacks of any treatment offered.
- *Informed consent*—patients have all the information they need to make a decision
- *Competence*—patients are competent to understand information and make a decision in their best interests.
- *Autonomy*—a patient has the right to accept or reject treatment.
- *Dignity*—a patient's dignity should be respected at all times.

Applying Principles

Although the principles may not appear controversial, their application is not always easy or straightforward, especially in complex cases involving life or death decisions. For example, how do doctors evaluate the risks of a treatment that has a low rate of success if the patient is certain to die without any treatment? Should a doctor expect a patient to undergo pain and suffering if a positive outcome is so unlikely? What if a patient wants to die, even if there is a good chance of success? And what does "dignity" really mean to a person who is in pain?

Deontology and Consequentialism

Medical ethics can work in different ethical frameworks. Two common opposing philosophies are called deontology and consequentialism. The basic premise of deontology (meaning duty) is that society operates around rules or duties that should never be broken. These rules may derive from religion or another ethical framework. To act morally, people should always obey the rules, even if the consequences are harmful. Consequentialism believes that actions should be judged by their outcomes (consequences), whether good or bad. A moral act is one that aims to produce the best outcomes.

It's a Fact

In 1992, the U.S. Joint Commission on the Accreditation of Healthcare Organizations said that all hospitals should put into place a means of addressing ethical concerns. In 1983, only 1 percent of U.S. hospitals had an ethics committee; by 1998, the figure was 90 percent. Today, every U.S. hospital has an ethics committee.

How does this relate to euthanasia? A deontological framework would state clear rules, for instance, "a doctor must always act to preserve life" or "a doctor must never act to deprive people of life, whatever their expressed wishes." In this framework, there is no possibility of euthanasia or assisted dying, however much someone suffers or however little possibility there is of the patient making a recovery. Critics say that although the rules of deontology may be clear, they are also rigid and show little understanding or compassion for people's situations. They also say that the outcomes can be harmful.

Consequentialists have rules, too, but these are not as rigid. A consequentialist framework looks at outcomes. For example, a consequentialist could argue that death may be the best outcome for a particular patient.

Consequentialists may ask if it is better to relieve someone's pain and suffering through death, rather than keep a patient alive at all costs? Are doctors respecting a patient's dignity or autonomy if they force the patient to undertake treatment that he or she does not want? Critics point out that it is impossible for doctors to know of the consequences of their actions and although they may think that they are doing good, the actual outcomes may be harmful.

▼ Practice makes perfect. Trainee medical staff must learn to resuscitate people whose hearts have stopped beating. Medical ethics say that a doctor must always act in the best interests of his or her patient.

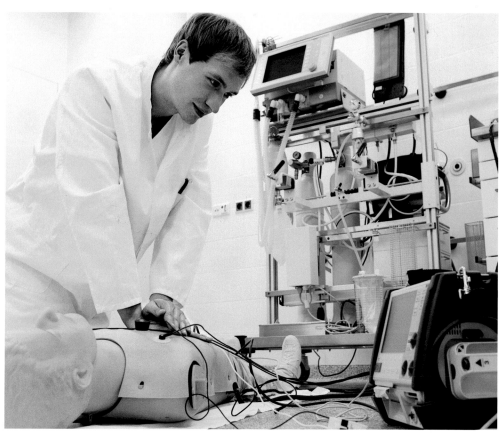

The Value of Life

How does the debate between deontology and consequentialism relate to medical ethics and euthanasia? It is useful to consider three issues that may come into conflict with each other, most simply expressed as "pro-life," "pro-mercy," and "pro-choice."

Pro-life is concerned with the issue of preserving life. Doctors should always try to do their best by a patient (benevolence) and avoid doing them harm (nonmaleficence). Normally, this means acting to save a patient's life. A deontologist would give a higher priority to the pro-life position in all circumstances, but a consequentialist would consider other issues in determining the right outcome.

"Pro-mercy" is concerned with a patient's pain and suffering and involves beneficence and nonmaleficence, as well as dignity and truthfulness. Doctors do not want to see their patients suffer, especially if it is for little gain—for example, a very elderly person or a person with a terminal illness who is already near the end of his or her life. Although such patients can be kept alive through medical intervention, this will increase their suffering. A deontologist believes that a doctor should keep the patient alive at any cost, but a consequentialist would argue that the ethical choice is to prevent the patient's pain and suffering, even if this results in death. Supporters of euthanasia would go farther and say that, at times, death is the best outcome and that medical ethics, therefore, should support euthanasia.

What happens when the pro-life and pro-mercy issues come into conflict? For instance, a doctor will try to relieve a patient's suffering by prescribing a strong painkiller, but by doing so, may hasten death. A deontologist might agree that this is permissible if the intention is to relieve suffering rather than to cause death. This position is now widely accepted in most systems of medical

▼ Truthfulness and informed consent are key principles of medical ethics, as is autonomy—the right of a patient to accept or reject treatment.

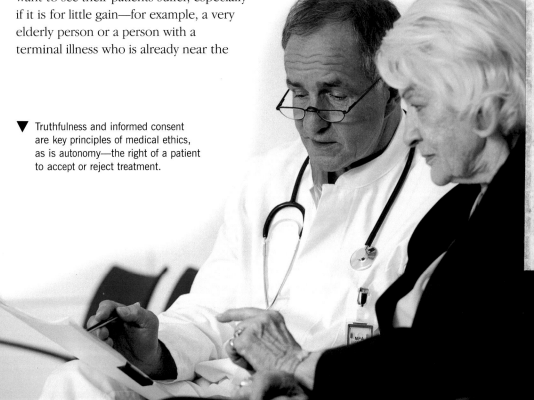

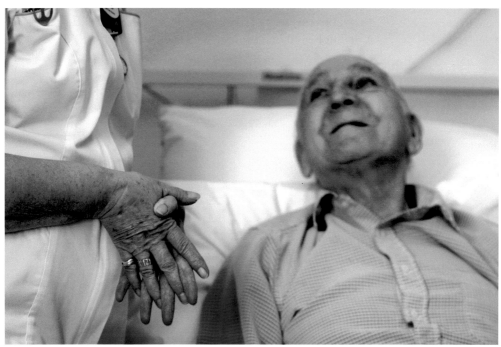

▲ The dignity of the patient is a key principle of medical ethics. This includes treating patients with respect and listening to their concerns.

ethics, including those approved by the Catholic Church. It is the intention rather than the outcome that is important. This is an example of what is known as the Doctrine of Double Effect.

Opponents of euthanasia say that some doctors hide behind the Doctrine of Double Effect when they use painkillers to bring about a patient's death and that this is a common practice for many doctors. However, others point out that with modern painkillers and better palliative care, the Doctrine of Double Effect is much less likely to be an ethical dilemma than it was in the past.

"Pro-choice" involves the principles of consent, competence, and autonomy. This is the most modern issue and reflects the changes in Western society whereby many people want, and expect, to take important decisions about their life and health, rather than leaving the decision to their doctors. For many people, making a decision about how and when they die is the most important choice of all. Some people spell out their wishes in a living will and others give instructions to their doctors or family members on what they want to happen in a critical situation.

For deontologists, this is a decision that the patient should not be able to make at all. They would question whether sick patients are really in a position to determine their best interests, especially on such a vital issue. A consequentialist may also question the decision but would not have such a rigid position and is likely to give the patient's wishes a higher value in determining the right outcome.

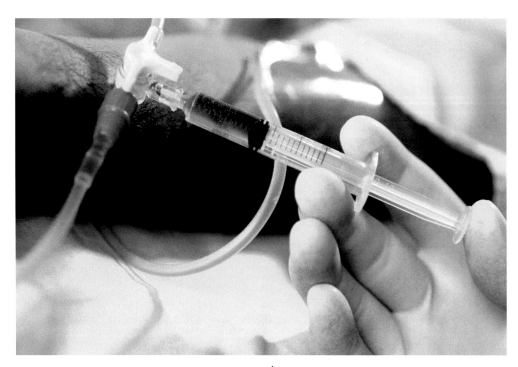

▲ A lethal drug is injected into a drip feed into the veins during an assisted suicide. This procedure is legal only in a few countries.

Quality of Life

One of the terms that appears again and again in the euthanasia debate is "quality of life." This is an ambiguous term, but generally, it refers to whether an individual can live in a way that is meaningful to himself or herself, and perhaps also to those they hold close.

What does this mean in practice? Does a person have to be conscious and aware of his or her surroundings? This is not true of a person in a PVS. Do patients have to be able to reason, feel emotions, or respond to stimuli? This is not always true of a severely disabled child. What happens if a person lives with intense or degenerative pain? This may affect many people suffering from a terminal or progressive illness, yet many would say that they still have a good quality of life.

What of old people with severe dementia? They may not know who or where they are, but still cling fiercely to life.

How is quality of life measured? People who are conscious and aware, even if they are in pain, can express their own views. Doctors should listen to their wishes, although they can refuse treatment if it is not clinically suitable or too risky—for example, surgeons should not operate if they feel that the patient is too frail to survive. Sometimes, doctors and patients agree to a "do not resuscitate" policy where, if the patient is on the verge of death, he or she will not be revived, even if the means are available. This can be controversial since the instinct of many doctors is to save life wherever possible. However, this is different from euthanasia or physician-assisted suicide, where the doctor actively helps the person to die.

But how do people ascertain the quality of life of someone in a persistent vegetative state, or someone who is otherwise unable to express themselves, such as a baby or a severely disabled child? Some people maintain that these latter groups can express themselves through facial expressions, sounds, or touch. Often, severely disabled people must rely on their families and carers to interpret their wishes. However, some people say that because carers are so involved and close to the patient, they cannot be objective and may not always give an accurate interpretation.

In these cases, doctors have to make difficult judgements. They must consider what the person's own wishes would be were he or she able to express them. Sometimes patients have expressed views before they became incapacitated or made a living will, although both can be unreliable. What are the views of the family members and carers, who know the person best? Is there a guardian or "independent advocate" whose role is to champion the person and consider his or her best interests? Ultimately, there is no objective standard of "quality of life" and doctors must rely on their own judgement.

Even people who are elderly, frail, and sick can cling fiercely to life. Modern medicine is often effective in helping to combat sickness and restoring people to health.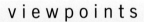

v i e w p o i n t s

"Whether you legalize it or decriminalize it or not, euthanasia was there, and is going to be there."
Dr. John Bos, retired oncologist from the Netherlands, with experience of performing euthanasia under the law

"We cannot entrust anyone—ourselves included—with absolute power. That is one of the reasons why I am opposed to such developments as voluntary euthanasia. It suggests that we are trustworthy, morally innocent, fundamentally good persons."
Dr.. Peter Jensen, Anglican Archbishop of Sydney, 2008

The Slippery Slope

One of the most common arguments against euthanasia is that it will inevitably lead to a situation where it is used more widely and indiscriminately. This is known as "the slippery slope."

The slippery slope argument is based on a deontologist view of ethics—rules that should never be broken, however difficult the circumstances. This states that broken rules inevitably lead to abuse. For example, a doctor may reluctantly agree not to treat a terminally ill person to allow for a peaceful death rather than prolonged suffering, but this will set a precedent for other cases. As time goes by, the doctor may agree to other requests, eventually, actively assisting a person to die. The doctor, rather than being a healer, becomes an agent of death.

Opponents of euthanasia quote cases of doctors who have overstepped the boundaries. One of the most notorious was Dr. Harold Shipman, a British general practitioner (family doctor), who killed over 200 elderly patients by lethal injections of the drug diamorphine. In 2006, a German nurse, Stephan Letter, was convicted of killing 29 patients with lethal cocktails of drugs. Supporters of euthanasia point out that these men were criminals who killed for self-gratification. Their actions should not be used as an argument \against euthanasia but for better regulation and oversight of the medical profession.

Opponents also say that once people accept euthanasia, however limited the circumstances, it is the beginning of a slippery slope that can lead to mass murder, as happened in Nazi Germany (see page 32). They point to more recent genocides such as Cambodia and Rwanda as examples of what happens to a society when all restraints break down.

Many people feel that these are extreme examples and have little relevance to euthanasia today, which focuses on individual choice in limited circumstances and with strict safeguards. They point out that Nazi Germany was a dictatorship that perverted medical ethics and lacked an independent legal system to challenge the government or independent media to bring attention to abuses. Both Cambodia and Rwanda were poor and war-torn countries where extremists were able to gain power, persecute their opponents,

◀ A mass grave from the "killing fields" of Cambodia is uncovered. From 1975 to 1979, the dictatorial Khmer Rouge believed in killing particular groups of people, including monks, educated people, city dwellers, and ethnic minorities. The Khmer Rouge is estimated to have killed between 1 and 2 million people.

case study

Helen

Helen was an 85-year-old widow living in Oregon, who had a history of breast cancer. She had a mastectomy (breast removal) but when the cancer recurred, she refused treatment, having seen her husband suffer a lingering death.

When she requested physician-assisted suicide under the terms of the Oregon Death with Dignity Act, she was frail but mentally alert and emotionally composed. Helen said that she expected no further value from her life. She did not see the point in additional personal indignities or in burdening her family with care, because in her mind, her life was already over. She wanted to be able to choose the moment to leave the world, when she was properly prepared and had said her farewells.

Helen talked with two doctors. Both were sympathetic but neither felt that they could assist her to end her life. The first had moral objections to the Death with Dignity Act, believing that doctors should not participate in assisted dying. The second felt that Helen's fear of pain prevented her from enjoying her remaining time and suggested that palliative care was the most appropriate treatment.

Helen and her family met a third doctor who agreed to help. They discussed her wishes and the legal requirements were set in motion. After a psychiatric assessment of her competence and mood, it was confirmed that she was not depressed and a second opinion confirmed that her cancer was terminal. The doctor prescribed the medication and Helen and her family began planning for her death.

and initiate mass killings. They say that such things would not happen in a stable and democratic society.

Some opponents of euthanasia agree that it is an exaggeration to see the slippery slope leading to mass extermination. They use more subtle arguments. They point out that medicine has many gray areas. They fear that if people allow any form of euthanasia, even with strict safeguards, then they push the boundaries of medical ethics and erode respect for human life. Rather than empowering individuals to make decisions about their death, euthanasia will be used on old, disabled, and vulnerable people who have no power to protest or fight for their rights.

summary

▶ Medical ethics are principles that govern a doctor's relationship with his or her patients.

▶ Different philosophical approaches, including deontology and consequentialism, guide doctors in deciding how to apply medical ethics, including whether to save life at all costs or to allow or assist people to die.

▶ It is extremely difficult to measure a person's "quality of life," especially if they are terminally ill or in pain.

▶ Some people regard euthanasia as a "slippery slope" that can result in indiscriminate killing.

CHAPTER 3

Choice and Control

While medical ethics guide doctors in their decision making, there are other factors, such as religion and the law, that influence whether euthanasia takes place.

Religion and Euthanasia

Religion is a driving force in many societies. Sometimes it has been the most important factor, ruling every aspect of people's lives and deaths. Even when religious practice has been frowned upon or banned by governments, people have performed religious rites at home or in private ceremonies. Today, in some countries, religion has a less important place and in secular Western countries, it is often seen as a largely private matter.

Religious leaders have a public platform and their views on controversial issues, such as contraception, abortion, and euthanasia, carry considerable weight.

No major religion allows euthanasia and many, although not all, of the people who speak out against euthanasia have strong religious beliefs. Most would agree that life is sacred and that euthanasia should not be permitted.

On the other hand, for some people, religion is not so important. They may be married or buried in religious ceremonies but religion plays little part in their daily lives. Others are agnostics or atheists, although their ethical framework might still be influenced by religion. In general, these people are likely to value individual choice and autonomy over traditional religious and moral frameworks. Many supporters of euthanasia have a strong secular outlook. They want the choice to die in certain circumstances, for example, if they are suffering from an incurable disease or a debilitating condition.

◀ Muslim worshipers prostrate themselves in prayer at a mosque. Like most religions, Islam says that life is sacred and forbids euthanasia.

Teenagers Marta Shkermanova (center) and Kristina Patrina (back) were convicted of killing their neighbor in Rostov on Don, Russia. The girls said that their neighbor had asked them to kill her because of the constant pain she suffered after a car crash. The girls were each given a prison sentence.

The Law and Euthanasia

In many Western countries, it is the law, rather than religion, that regulates people's behavior, at least in the public sector. Many legal systems are still influenced by religious beliefs, either implicitly or explicitly. Legal systems change over time, especially as governments pass new laws in response to and influenced by public opinion. As a result, some countries and states have passed laws that allow for some forms of euthanasia.

Doctors must act within the law while following ethical principles and acting in the best interests of their patients. In most cases, there will be no conflict, but in issues of life and death, there may be a thin line between the two. In these cases, doctors consult their colleagues and hospital ethics committees, as well as the patient and his or her family members. However, many doctors say they will always act with caution to avoid breaking the law, even in situations where the law is unclear. Many fear that they will face disciplinary procedures or a lawsuit, which will affect their own life, their hospital, and their other patients.

All countries have laws against killing. For opponents of euthanasia, this alone can act as proof of the wrongness of euthanasia. Killing is murder and there should be no exceptions. However, in the late twentieth and early twenty-first century, a few countries, such as Albania and the Netherlands, have passed laws or established practices that allow euthanasia under certain, strict conditions. These laws are invariably controversial and are often challenged.

It's a Fact

Between 2003 and 2006, Lord Joel Joffe made four attempts to introduce a Patient Assisted Dying Bill in the House of Lords in the UK. The bill would give doctors the right to prescribe drugs that terminally ill patients in severe pain could take to end their life. The bill had supporters and opponents in all parties, inside and outside parliament. A Special Committee was established to examine the bill, but it was defeated in 2006.

The Case of Oregon and the Netherlands

Countries or states that have passed laws permitting euthanasia in some form include Switzerland (1942), the state of Oregon (1994), Albania (1999), the Netherlands (2001), Belgium (2002), Thailand (2007), and Luxembourg (2008). Between 1996 and 1997, euthanasia was legalized in Australia's Northern Territory. Japan has no law regarding euthanasia, but legal judgements allow it under certain conditions.

Oregon became the first and so far the only U.S. state to allow "physician-assisted dying" under certain conditions through its Death with Dignity Act of 1994. The law came into being through a state ballot (Proposition 16). The resulting vote was close, with 51.3 percent in favor and 48.7 percent against. An additional ballot in 1997 failed to overturn the Act and it has since been confirmed as valid by the U.S. Supreme Court.

The Death with Dignity Act allows an adult, who is resident in Oregon and who is diagnosed with a terminal illness that will result in death within six months, to request their doctor to administer medication that will lead to death. The patient must be judged as capable (that is, must understand their situation, and not be clinically depressed or mentally ill). The request must be confirmed by two witnesses, one of whom must be an independent witness. The patient's medical records must also be inspected by a second doctor. After the request for death has been agreed, the patient must wait another 15 days, and make a second, oral request. Only then can the doctor go ahead with the request.

The Netherlands follows a middle course. The government there recognized that for many years, some doctors had been assisting terminally ill patients to die, a practice that seemed to have public acceptance. The Termination of Life on Request and Assisted Suicide Act stated that doctors who assisted a patient to die would not be prosecuted if certain conditions were followed. The patient must be suffering from a long-term or terminal illness or be in intolerable pain.

◀ Anti-euthanasia demonstrators in Hanover, Germany, protest against the decision of the Swiss euthanasia organization, Dignitas, to open a branch in the city. Euthanasia is legal in Switzerland but illegal in Germany, so German residents wishing for an assisted death have to travel to Switzerland where euthanasia is legal, although still controversial.

case study

Graeme Wylie

Did Graeme Wylie really want to die? Was he capable of making a rational decision? These were questions considered by a jury in Sydney, Australia, in 2008. Mr. Wylie's partner, Shirley Justons, and his friend, Caren Jenning, were on trial, charged with causing his death.

The case was complex. Mr. Wylie was diagnosed with Alzheimer's disease in 2003. Alzheimer's disease causes memory loss and confusion. Although it is not a life-threatening condition, it can result in the disintegration of an individual's personality, making the sufferer completely dependent on others for care.

In 2005, acting on behalf of Mr. Wylie, Ms. Justons approached the Swiss euthanasia organization, Dignitas, to request legally assisted suicide. His two adult daughters reluctantly supported the request. However, Dignitas rejected the request because of concerns over Wylie's mental capacity. His daughters then withdrew their support.

In 2006, Ms. Jenning returned from Mexico with a supply of the drug Nembutal, banned for nonveterinary use in Australia. In March 2006, Ms. Justons helped Mr. Wylie to die by giving him the drug. At first, she said that she had no idea what had happened to Mr. Wylie, but she was later arrested for murder. During the trial, she pleaded guilty to assisted suicide.

The trial looked at the possible motives for the women to cause Mr. Wylie's death. Was it in response to his wishes, as they both maintained, or was it for financial reasons? Both women were members of Exit International, a pro-euthanasia group.

In June 2008, the jury decided that Graeme Wylie did not take his own life. They found Shirley Justons guilty of manslaughter. Caren Jenning was found guilty of being an accessory to manslaughter. The case attracted much public and media attention at a time when several Australian states were considering legalizing euthanasia under certain conditions.

The doctor must be the patient's own doctor, must continuously consult with the patient on his or her wishes, and must be convinced that the patient really wishes to die and that death is in his or her best interests. A second doctor must be consulted and must agree with the course of action. The doctor must follow agreed procedures to bring about death, and afterward report these actions to the public prosecutor. The law can still act against a doctor if the rules have been broken, but this is rare.

For supporters of euthanasia, Oregon and the Netherlands are examples of good and humane practice. There are strong safeguards in place to prevent abuse, and clinical judgement is given a proper place in the procedure. The doctor has a long-term, trusting relationship with the patient who has many opportunities to step back from the final act. But opponents disagree. They say that the Oregon system was pushed through by a bare majority of voters and that the Netherlands situation is a license for doctors to act with impunity.

Can the Patient Choose?

Many of those who support euthanasia say that ultimately the decision must be the patient's own. Individuals are best placed to understand their own situation, consider their own best interests and determine if, when, and how they want to die. Supporters argue that this is consistent with the medical principles of dignity and autonomy (see page 12).

Do patients always know their best interests and can they correctly express their wishes? People considering euthanasia are usually terminally ill, very sick, or in severe pain. They may be depressed or confused, lonely, or frightened. Opponents of euthanasia say that rather than giving sick people dignity and autonomy, having to make such a decision places them under intolerable strain. If people believe that their situation is hopeless, then they are more likely to opt for death rather than life.

Living Wills

Some people express their wishes through living wills, but these are not always recognized by doctors or the courts. However, in most cases, they are given considerable weight, at least in cases involving "do not resuscitate" notices or withdrawal of life support, where death is imminent or inevitable. Many people would say that this is not euthanasia, but accepting the right of a person to die in dignity, without ineffective medical intervention.

What of the situation of the majority of people who do not make living wills? For young people especially, death seems very distant. Sometimes individuals may have spoken of their wishes to others. However, in most cases, these are not expressed in a considered or consistent way—it might be someone remembering a remark such as "if that happens to me, I do not want to live." People also make contradictory statements at different times and to different people.

The most extreme cases involve people, such as Terri Schiavo (see page 4) or Tony Bland (page 31), living in a long-term persistent vegetative state. Both were young people, whose incapacity came without warning. How much can people rely on wishes, if any, that an individual had expressed before becoming unconscious? It could be argued that once a person is unconscious, his or her previous wishes are no longer valid.

Some people feel that if patients are not in a position to make a rational choice, family members should be able to make a decision on their behalf. Parents of very sick babies or young children may request the withholding of medical treatment if they feel that it will be unduly intrusive,

▲ A judge considers evidence in one of the many court cases of Terri Schiavo (see page 4). The lawyer (right) represented Michael Schiavo, Terri's husband.

painful, or experimental and will not benefit the children, either by extending their life or improving their quality of life. However, these requests may be challenged by health authorities or the courts.

Family members do have an important role to play and are consulted by doctors on end-of-life issues. However, there are cases, such as Terri Schiavo (see page 4), where family members disagree with each other. Opponents also point out that family members may be influenced by factors other than the best interests of the patient, such as ridding themselves of a "burden" or gaining an inheritance or insurance payouts. However, supporters say that these cases are easily weeded out and that the vast majority of families aim to act in the best interest of their loved ones.

summary

▶ Religious belief is a major factor in determining people's views on euthanasia—most religions are opposed to euthanasia.

▶ Euthanasia is not legal in most countries and doctors must act within the law.

▶ Euthanasia in certain circumstances is allowed in some countries—these include Switzerland, the Netherlands, Belgium, and the state of Oregon.

▶ Some people are able to express their own views on treatment, including euthanasia, or draw up living wills.

CHAPTER 4

Pushing Back the Barriers

"The days of our lives are three score years and 10," so says the King James Bible. Not so long ago, 70 was considered to be a "good age"—most people did not live that long. Consider life expectancy in the United States. In 1900, at birth, a white man could expect to live 47 years, and an African-American man only 33 years; a white women might live to 49 and an African-American women to 34. Census figures 100 years later revealed a dramatic change. White men could expect to live to 75, African-American men to 68, white women to 80, and African-American women to 75.

Life expectancy in other countries is even higher. For example, in Japan, men can expect to live to 78 years of age and women until 85 years old, and thousands reach 100 years old or more. The main reasons behind this change are rising living standards, fewer wars, and better medical care. Once, surgeons were reluctant to prescribe new drugs or to operate on older people, but today, these treatments are routinely offered. Some procedures, such as artificial hip replacements and heart operations, give older people more years of active life.

◀ More people are living into old age today than at any other time in history. Many say that these are the best years of their lives

Old Age

An aging population brings its own problems. Not all older people remain in good health—they become frailer physically and mentally, and may need extra care. Others become depressed and lonely when spouses, family members, and friends die as the years pass. Many older people fear losing their faculties and becoming dependent on others, perhaps spending years in a hospital bed or nursing home. Although many people retain a zest for life to the end, others feel that they have lived enough and just want to have "a good death."

Some people question whether expensive medical resources should be spent giving frail and elderly people a few extra months of life. However, to counter this argument, others point out that older people have contributed to society and have earned the right to good medical care.

▲ Sickness and disability affect the lives of some elderly people and can severely damage their quality of life.

Supporters of euthanasia say that many older people do not want to live on into a frail and painful old age and that they should have the right to choose when they die. However, opponents argue this move would be extremely dangerous. It could lead to older people who are depressed choosing to die rather than seeking treatment that could improve their physical and mental wellbeing. It could also enable doctors or relatives to influence the person to make this decision. Critics say that older people need protection and support, not assisted dying.

It's a Fact

In the United States, the senior population is getting older. In 1997, the 65–74 age group (18.5 million) was eight times larger than it was in 1900, but the 75–84 group (11.7million) was 16 times larger and the 85-plus group (3.9 million) was 31 times larger.

▲ A premature baby lies in a neonatal unit. Intensive care has saved the lives of many babies who would once have died at or before birth.

The Beginning of Life

Medical advances have also resulted in dramatic interventions at the beginning of life. Not so long ago, childbirth itself was a perilous process, for both the mother and the baby. This is still the case in many less economically developed countries, where the United Nations Population Fund estimates that each year, over half a million women die as a result of pregnancy and birth.

Babies in wealthier countries have much better chances of living than in the past. Most are delivered safely by doctors and midwives. Children are vaccinated against diseases that once killed, and sicknesses and infections are diagnosed and treated. Tests such as ultrasound scans mean that some conditions can be detected while the baby is still in the womb.

There has been huge improvement in the survival of very premature babies. Even 20 years ago, it was rare for babies born before 30 weeks (three-quarters of the gestation period) to survive. Today, new drugs, sophisticated equipment, and round-the-clock specialist care mean that premature babies have much better chances of survival. For instance, one UK study found that around 36 percent of 25-week babies survived to be sent home between 1994–1999 and this had risen to 47 percent in 2005. However, babies below 24 weeks had very low rates of survival and these had not improved over the same period.

Why is the survival rate so low? Doctors believe that technology can do only so much. When a baby's lungs, heart, and brain are so underdeveloped at birth, it is impossible to properly catch up. Of those babies who do survive, many are disabled, often severely, or in pain.

Many doctors question whether such babies will have a good quality of life. They point out that although premature babies receive excellent intensive care while they are in a hospital, the level of care is likely to diminish once they go home. All too often, a family finds itself trying to cope with a child with very high care needs. However much they love their child, parents may wonder whether it was right to keep them alive at all costs, rather than let them die soon after birth, which would have happened in the past.

However, there are arguments on the other side. Many people feel that all life is valuable and that everything should be done to save very premature babies, whatever the cost. They argue that the problem is not the disability but society's attitudes. If society really valued disabled people, it would provide the help and support that is needed. As for the quality-of-life argument, they say that severely disabled children can enjoy life and express themselves through gesture, touch, and facial expression.

▼ Children with physical or learning disabilities can still have a good quality of life if they receive care and attention, like these children at a children's center in Bulgaria.

Between Life and Death

The area of medical intervention that has produced the most publicized cases of euthanasia has been that of people suspended between life and death. Medical technologies can now keep people alive if they are unconscious, in a coma, or physically paralyzed. Is it right to prolong life long beyond natural boundaries?

The most controversial issues involve people whose brains have been damaged but whose basic body functions remain working with outside support. They may be able to blink, breathe on their own, move their limbs, and smile, cry, or laugh, although not as an emotional response to events. They retain some functions in their lower brain (which controls their breathing and blood circulation), but some or all of their higher brain (their thoughts, emotions, personality) has been damaged.

Researchers distinguish between people who are in a PVS who show no signs of conscious behavior, and people in a minimally conscious state (MCS) who retain some consciousness, however limited and inconsistent. Sometimes the

patient will make a full or partial recovery but the longer the condition continues, the less likely a person is to recover. A patient with MCS may eventually recover, whereas one with PVS will never recover. For some family members, the suspended state gives a chance to say goodbye before death, but others refuse to give up—they believe that there will be a recovery however long it takes. A person may stay alive in PVS for months or years, until his or her body functions stop naturally. It is often argued that euthanasia is a right and appropriate course for patients in PVS. Supporters of euthanasia say that PVS sufferers are in effect dead, their body is kept alive only because of artificial feeding or medical intervention, there is no dignity and no quality of life. For family members, the strain can be terrible. Without a death, they cannot grieve or move on, and they may face financial strain or complex legal issues. Supporters say that keeping someone alive under these circumstances is unethical.

Others argue that life is sacred and should be safeguarded in all circumstances. No doubt death may be convenient for some family members, but most do not want to see their loved one die. On a practical level, opponents point out that making an accurate diagnosis is very difficult and there have been people diagnosed with PVS who were later discovered to have MCS and gone on to make a recovery. Death is a final step and if an error has been made, life can never return.

Tony Bland

Tony Bland's life changed for ever on April 15, 1989, when he was one of hundreds of fans crushed in an overcrowded football stadium in Sheffield, England. Tony did not die that day but was severely injured and the oxygen flow to his brain was interrupted. He never recovered consciousness.

Tony's family spent months at his bedside, hoping for some sign of life. Neurologists discovered that his brain was permanently damaged and had no function at all. However, artificial feeding and expert nursing kept his body alive and he was classed as being in a PVS.

Tony's doctor consulted his family on their wishes. There was no possibility of Tony ever recovering or improving. His family decided that the food and water that was keeping him alive should be withdrawn. However, since the doctor might be charged with murder, the hospital asked the courts to rule on the case. Since Tony could not speak for himself, the court appointed a guardian to represent him. The Official Solicitor, representing the government, opposed the application. The court decided that the hospital could withdraw treatment, but the case was considered so important the government was allowed to appeal. The doctors who testified stated that Tony would never recover. In the end, the Court of Appeal allowed the original decision to stand.

Tony died on March 3, 1994, 10 days after doctors withdrew life-saving support. He was just 22 and had spent almost four years unconscious in the hospital. He was the first person in British legal history to be allowed to die by the courts as a result of the withdrawal of treatment. Between 1994 and 2000, 18 similar cases were considered by courts in England and Wales.

▲ An anti-euthanasia protester stands outside the hospital where Tony Bland had received treatment and eventually died.

summary

▶ People are living much longer lives but this creates new health problems and extra spending on medical resources.

▶ Medical advances result in more premature babies being saved and more disabled children with high care needs.

▶ The most publicized cases of euthanasia concern people in a persistent vegetative state (PVS).

CHAPTER 5

Disabled or Dead?

Many disabled people oppose euthanasia because they fear that it would be used against them, either as babies, children, or adults. They point to cases where governments have followed policies that have resulted in the killing, maiming, or neglect of people with disabilities.

Nazi Germany

The most extreme and notorious example was the T-4 euthanasia program conducted by the National Socialist (Nazi) regime in Germany from 1933–45. From the beginning, the Nazis, led by Adolf Hitler, routinely imprisoned their political enemies, Jews and Roma (gypsies). Since they preached "racial purity" and praised physical perfection, it was not surprising that they saw people with physical and mental disabilities and mental illnesses as enemies.

In 1938, Hitler authorized the T-4 program to remove children with learning difficulties from homes and to close the religious and charitable institutions that looked after them. Some children were then subjected to so-called medical experiments, others were starved or killed outright. Later, the program moved on to the killing of disabled adults, first in Germany and then in the conquered countries. There was some opposition within Germany. Families hid disabled children to prevent them being taken away.

▼ Nazi propaganda depicted disabled children as burdens to their family and society. The aim was to prepare the public for their removal from their families and death.

The Catholic Church bravely denounced the T-4 program. In 1941, Bishop von Galen of Munster said in a sermon: "We are talking about men and women, our compatriots, our brothers and sisters. Poor, unproductive people if you wish, but does this mean that they have lost their right to live?" Nevertheless, by the end of the war, it is estimated that the program had killed hundreds of thousands of disabled children and adults. Later, some of those responsible were tried and sentenced by the Allied War Crimes Tribunal.

For many disabled people, the policies practiced by the Nazis are an extreme version of the discrimination and prejudice that they continue to face worldwide. They say that any acceptance of euthanasia will result in it being used against disabled people whose lives are not valued by mainstream society.

Supporters of euthanasia also condemn Nazi policies but emphasize that these were crimes against humanity, and have nothing in common with the term euthanasia as it is used today. They point out that the T-4 program was a system of state-sanctioned mass murder designed to eliminate vulnerable people, whereas euthanasia is about supporting an individual's right to choose to die, in specific and carefully defined circumstances.

Opponents say that any policy that authorizes euthanasia, however limited the circumstances, will always be a threat to disabled people. The fact that such campaigns were used in the past shows that they could also be used in the future.

▲ Bishop von Galen, the Catholic bishop of Munster, spoke out publicly against the T-4 program that killed hundreds of thousands of disabled people. After the war, he was made a Cardinal and long after this death, given the title Blessed.

viewpoints

"The proposed law is only for terminally ill people, not disabled people. Disabled people who have lived with disability all their lives and fight for equal rights are in a better position to withstand pressure. Why should they suddenly crack in the last six months of their life?"

Lord Joel Joffe, UK campaigner for voluntary euthanasia

"The current debate about euthanasia has made some terrible assumptions about the quality of disabled people's lives. It has rarely included the voices of disabled people and their right to live, and we must see the balance redressed."

Liz Sayce, Director of Policy, UK Disability Rights Commission, 2003

Disability Is Not Death

Over the past 50 years, disabled people have founded organizations to promote their human rights. One of their distinguishing features has been their insistence on speaking for themselves, rather than letting others speak on their behalf. They have demanded that governments and the medical profession listen to their concerns.

Disabled people's organizations say that their lives are often considered to be of less value than an able-bodied person and that they are not treated equally. One example is children with Down Syndrome, who often have heart problems. Once, these children were seen as having severely limited lives. Today, many people born with Down Syndrome go to school or college and hold down jobs. However, for a long time, they were routinely denied the heart surgery that could prolong their lives, although this was available to able-bodied children. Today, this is much less likely to happen, thanks to campaigning by disabled people's organizations and their supporters.

Nevertheless, many disabled people say that they do not receive equal medical treatment, especially in critical situations. For example, they are less likely to be given life-saving treatment, even when they clearly state their wishes to do so, but instead receive "do not resuscitate" notices. They say that most doctors judge them as having a poor quality of life, simply because they are disabled. This reflects general attitudes in society that their lives are inferior and that it is better to be dead than disabled.

The disability movement has been one of the most outspoken opponents of any moves to legalize or otherwise recognize euthanasia. Members say that it is wrong for society to judge their lives as inferior because they are disabled and that even if people are in extreme pain, then death is not the answer. They say that by recognizing euthanasia, disabled people will inevitably become its chief victims. This is the start of the "slippery slope" (see pages 18–19), whereby euthanasia starts as "mercy killing" of disabled people in pain and then extends to routine dismissal of disabled people's rights and concerns.

Opponents of euthanasia say that this is especially the case in countries where healthcare is not free and where medical treatment is expensive. In these situations, disabled people can be made to feel that they are a heavy financial burden on their families. There are fears that they can be pressured into accepting cheaper,

◀ A little boy with Down Syndrome enjoys playing with toys at nursery school. Once, such children were seen as unable to benefit from education, but today, they attend school with other children.

case study

Dame Jane Campbell

Jane Campbell is a British social reformer and campaigner for disabled people's rights.
She is a founder of the Center for Independent Living and is a Commissioner of the British government's Human Rights and Equality Commission.

Jane was born with spinal muscular atrophy, but leads an active life with the help of a wheelchair, breathing aid, and computer. In January 2003, she was rushed to the hospital with severe pneumonia in both lungs. The consultant who was treating her said: "I presume that if you go into respiratory failure that you will not want to be resuscitated on a ventilator." When she asked why, the consultant said that the chances of her living without the ventilator would be remote—and "I wouldn't want to live like that." When Jane said that refusing resuscitation would mean that she would die and that of course she wanted to be ventilated, the consultant backed down.

The following day, when Jane was in intensive care, another consultant said the same thing. By now, she was very worried. Her husband went home and returned with a photograph of Jane in her graduation gown receiving her doctorate. He pushed the picture before the doctors: "Look, this is my wife, not what you think she is and has become. You should do everything for her that you would do for anybody in this situation. She is young and has everything to live for." The doctors changed their minds and followed her wishes. Jane Campbell later said: "Surely such measures should not be needed to access life-saving treatment. This should be my right—a right to life."

In 2006, Jane became a politician in the House of Lords, part of the British Parliament. Now as Dame Jane Campbell, she uses her position to campaign against attempts to legalize euthanasia in the UK.

---

inferior treatment or no treatment at all, in effect, condemning them to certain death. Opponents say that this is euthanasia by the back door.

However, supporters of euthanasia say that disability organizations misrepresent the modern euthanasia movement, which does not target disabled people, but rather supports individual choice in specific and limited circumstances. Furthermore, the disability movement does not speak for everyone who is sick or disabled—people are individuals and all have the right to make their own decisions.

summary

▶ The Nazis used the T-4 extermination program to kill thousands of disabled children and adults.

▶ Disabled people have faced discrimination in medical care.

▶ Disabled people's organizations oppose euthanasia saying that it will be directed against disabled people.

CHAPTER 6

Dying with Dignity

One of the most commonly used phrases in the euthanasia debate is "dying with dignity." For supporters of euthanasia, this usually means a death that is not only peaceful and painless, but which also has an element of choice as to the time, place, and method of death. Opponents agree that a peaceful and painless death is the ideal, but that maintaining the quality of a person's natural life is more important.

Choice and Palliative Care

For many people, death is unexpected and painful. Each year, 400,000 young people under the age of 25 die in road accidents worldwide. Others die from infectious diseases, cancers, and heart conditions. There is no choice in these deaths, although many lives could be saved if rapid and effective treatment were available.

Supporters of euthanasia point to the Netherlands. There, most people who choose euthanasia die at home, having said farewell to family and friends, tended to by their family doctor. Their death is usually peaceful and painless amid familiar surroundings.

Opponents of euthanasia reply that improved palliative care has removed the need for any sick person to ask their doctor to help them die. Palliative care is not about cure but about relieving pain and suffering and providing a good quality of life. It includes pain management, often through a carefully controlled intake of drugs or assistance with feeding or

◀ Death can come suddenly and without warning. Road accidents continue to be a major killer worldwide.

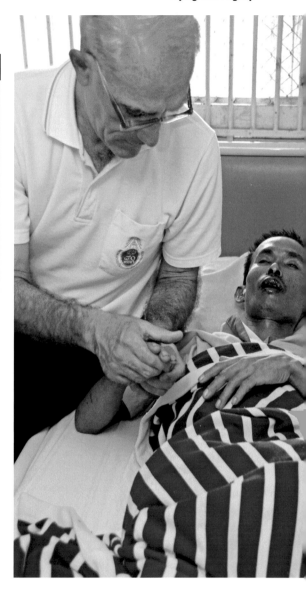

▲ A man dying from AIDS in Thailand is comforted by Father Michael Bassano, an American priest who volunteers at a Buddhist temple that houses a hospice for AIDS patients, offering palliative care.

breathing. The aim is for the patient to be comfortable and to support the patient's family as death approaches. Palliative care is given in hospitals, hospices, nursing homes, and increasingly, patients' own homes.

Supporters of euthanasia say that they welcome the advances in palliative care, but that euthanasia should still be an option when this fails. They point out that Oregon, where euthanasia is legal, also has good quality and widely available palliative care. One study showed that of the hundreds people who applied to die under Oregon's Death with Dignity Act, all but one had accepted the offer of palliative care. This also seems to be the case in the Netherlands where numbers of euthanasia deaths have fallen.

Opponents of euthanasia say that this is a false picture and that euthanasia itself can be painful. Drugs do not always work quickly or effectively. In extreme cases, as with patients in a PVS, euthanasia can result in days of starvation or dehydration, although this can also be lessened through drugs. For supporters of euthanasia, these problems are reasons for better medication and improved pain relief being more widely available before and during euthanasia.

Living with Pain

Some of the individuals who have been most vocal in their support of euthanasia are people who are affected with degenerative conditions or terminal illnesses. These include motor neurone disease, multiple sclerosis, and some types of cancer.

These are particularly cruel conditions because although modern medicine can diagnose the disease and keep people alive for longer, it has not yet been able to provide a cure or prevent suffering. For many people, these are welcome developments. However, others see it as a living death. They know that their condition will inevitably worsen, that their body will become weaker and their bodily functions will fail, and they will become dependent on others, and often upon machines such as ventilators to assist their breathing. Under such circumstances, they decide that some may want to end their lives at a time and place of their choosing, rather than be kept alive whatever the cost and whatever the circumstances.

For some people, it is the pain they experience that blights their life. Although they are alive, they can no longer take any pleasure in their surroundings. They see euthanasia as a way to end the pain. Opponents of euthanasia point to the improvements in palliative care and new painkilling techniques. Supporters reply that these are not always effective, and in any case, many people do not want to spend their last weeks or months in a drug-induced state.

Other people say that it is not pain that is the main problem. After all, many have lived with pain for a long time. Rather, it is the loss of dignity and autonomy that

prompts their wish to die. They no longer feel like a whole person and are totally dependent upon others to fulfill even their basic needs. They contend that euthanasia would enable them to die with dignity. Some people say that they would commit suicide but no longer have the physical ability, and without legalized euthanasia, any requests to their doctor or family for assistance places those who agree to help in jeopardy since they could be charged with murder or assisting a suicide.

Opponents of euthanasia say that however difficult the circumstances, people should not be allowed the right to choose to die. People in these terrible circumstances are not always capable of making a rational decision. Even more importantly, it is the beginning of a slippery slope, because if people with degenerative diseases or terminal conditions are allowed to make the decision to die, then there will be pressure to extend the right to other groups, who are even more dependent or vulnerable.

case study

Diane Petty

Diane Petty was a British woman who was diagnosed with motor neurone disease (MND) when she was 40. MND is an incurable degenerative disease where the nerve cells that control the muscles are slowly destroyed. Ultimately, sufferers are unable to walk, speak, breathe, or swallow by themselves.

Within four months, Diane was using a wheelchair and was dependent on her family for all her needs. Her pain was so severe that she asked her husband to help her end her life. However, euthanasia and assisted suicide are illegal in Britain. In August 2001, Petty wrote to the Director of Public Prosecutions (DPP) asking that her husband, Brian, be given immunity from prosecution if he helped her to commit suicide.

The DPP refused to grant immunity. This was the beginning of a legal process that saw Mrs. Petty take her case to the courts, first to the High Court in London, then to a review by the Law Lords (the British equivalent of the Supreme Court). Both courts said that UK law was not ready to sanction the idea of assisted suicide. The final step was to petition the European Court of Human Rights. Although she was in great pain, in March 2002, she traveled for 12 hours to attend the hearing. A month later, the European judges rejected her appeal.

Diane's situation aroused great sympathy in Britain. Some Members of Parliament called for a change in the law. A television documentary followed her trip to Strasbourg. However, not everyone agreed with her wish, especially disabled people's organizations.

Diane Petty died in a hospice near her home on May 11, 2002. She had slipped into a coma after suffering breathing difficulties. Her husband said that he was proud of her and "glad that she was free at last."

◀ Although she was severely disabled, Diane Petty continued to campaign for her right to choose her own death.

summary

▶ Some people see euthanasia as a way of achieving a dignified death at a time of their choosing.

▶ People with terminal diseases or living in constant pain are some of the most vocal advocates of euthanasia.

▶ Opponents of euthanasia say that good palliative care means that there is no need for euthanasia.

CHAPTER 7

Society and Euthanasia Today

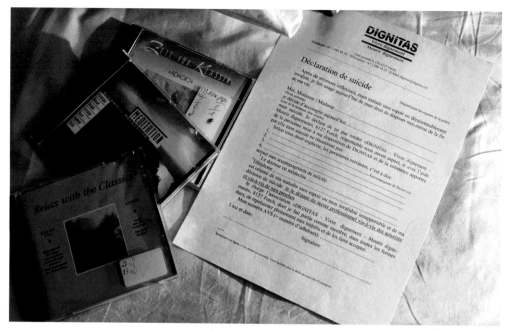

▲ Dignitas is an organization that supports people from all over the world to undertake assisted suicide in Switzerland, where euthanasia is legal.

Organizations promoting euthanasia were established in the early twentieth century as part of the eugenics movement. Eugenics focused on "improving" populations by weeding out "weaker" individuals (such as physically or mentally disabled children), mainly by selective breeding but sometimes through euthanasia. At the end of the World War II, the horror of the Nazi death camps (see page 32) meant that support for eugenics disappeared and there was little interest in euthanasia.

However, from the 1960s, medical advances and changing social attitudes saw the establishment of new pro-euthanasia movements in many countries. Many of

their ideas have entered into public debate, even in countries where euthanasia has little chance of being adopted in law.

Pro and Anti-euthanasia Organizations

Organizations supporting euthanasia are inevitably controversial. Most aim to inform the public debate and influence governments to legalize some forms of euthanasia under certain conditions. They see euthanasia as supporting individual choice, autonomy, and dignity. These organizations do not practice euthanasia or assist suicide, although some may refer individuals to other organizations that take a more active role.

Some pro-euthanasia organizations assist people to die. Their activities are illegal (with the exception of a few countries where euthanasia is legal, such as Switzerland) and highly controversial. The most publicized pro-euthanasia activist is Dr. Jack Kevorkian, a physician from Michigan. While practicing as a doctor, he claimed that his "suicide machine" enabled over 100 people to die. Although he was stripped of his medical degree and taken to court several times, Dr. Kevorkian could not be convicted of his patient's deaths since they had died by their own hand. However, in 1998, he allowed a movie showing him administering a lethal drug to a terminally ill man to be shown on a television documentary. He was tried and convicted of second-degree murder, serving eight years in jail before he was paroled in 2007. He agreed on his release not to practice euthanasia, although he still supports its legalization.

In response, organizations have been established to oppose euthanasia. They have gathered support from many people in the disability movement and in religious organizations, as well as some members of the medical profession. Many organizations describe themselves as "right to life" movements.

Some opponents see pro-euthanasia groups as direct descendants of the eugenics movement. They say that however much these organizations present themselves as supporters of individual choice, euthanasia will lead to a general acceptance of the deaths of "unwanted" people, such as sick and disabled people, who are seen as a burden to their families and costly to the health system. Other opponents acknowledge that euthanasia, under some conditions, might seem like a valid choice for a terminally ill individual, but fear that there will be a slow widening of the criteria, leading to a gentle but definitely slippery slope. They point out that even in the strictest system, doctors such as Dr. Kevorkian can behave unethically, and that some members of euthanasia movements have been charged and convicted of unlawful killings.

◀ Dr. Jack Kevorkian is an outspoken supporter of euthanasia and has actively assisted over 100 people to die. He was found guilty of second-degree murder and imprisoned.

Public Opinion on Euthanasia

There have been many public opinion polls on people's attitudes toward euthanasia and how these relate to existing laws. They seem to indicate that in many countries, most people would support euthanasia in some circumstances.

When the Dutch euthanasia law came into effect in 2002, surveys suggested that over 80 percent of the Dutch population supported the new law. At the same time, a public opinion poll in Belgium, which legalized euthanasia in 2002, found 72 percent of the population supporting some form of euthanasia. A German poll found that 64 percent of people in West Germany and 80 percent in East Germany felt that a critically ill patient should have a right to die. In France, 84 percent of those polled said that they would support euthanasia.

In the United States, the proportion of people in favor of euthanasia seems to be lower. For example, a Gallop Poll in May 2006 asked: "If a person has a disease that cannot be cured, should doctors be allowed by law to end the patient's life by some painless means if the patient and his family request it?" The poll found that 69 percent agreed, 27 percent disagreed, and 4 percent were unsure. Only 64 percent agreed that the doctor should be allowed to assist the patient to commit suicide, with 31 percent against. Some polls have shown lower percentages in favor (although still a majority). During the Terri Schiavo controversy (see page 4), opinion polls found that a majority supported her husband's decision to withdraw artificial feeding.

In January 2007, the British Attitudes Survey found that 80 percent of people would support a change in the law to allow

doctors to actively help people with a terminal illness who want to die. Some 60 percent of those questioned supported doctors prescribing drugs that patients could use to end their life. However, only 44 percent said that a family member should be permitted to help a terminally ill person to die. Only 33 percent said that physician-assisted suicide should be allowed for a person with an incurable, but not terminal, sickness. Less than 25 percent of those who answered the poll thought that it should be allowed when a person was not in severe pain or close to death but depended on carers for basic needs.

But opponents of euthanasia say that public opinion polls can be misleading, and depend largely on what questions are asked and the responses that are required. For example, people are often asked to give simple "yes" and "no" answers to complex questions. Also, people do not always understand the complexity of all the issues. In any case, an ethical issue such as euthanasia should be judged on its own terms, not by the outcome of public opinion polls.

case study

Janusz Switaj

Janusz Switaj was 18 when he was severely injured in a motorcycle accident that severed his spinal cord. He was left completely paralyzed. At first, he was in a coma and was kept alive on an artificial respirator.

In February 2007, when Janusz was 32 years old and had emerged from his coma, he had a letter written on his behalf to the local court in Warsaw, Poland. He said that he survived thanks only to the artificial respirator and to the round-the-clock care provided by his elderly parents in their small apartment. He said that he no longer had any "biological, psychological, social, or economic" grounds to live and that he wanted his life to be "cut short."

Euthanasia is not legal in Poland and the court could not approve his request.

Had Janusz awoken from the coma before the attachment of the respirator, legally, he would have been able to ask the doctors to provide no further treatment. However, once the machine was switched on, it could not be switched off since it would result in his death.

Janusz's letter was given considerable attention in the media. A survey found that 50 percent of those people polled thought that euthanasia should be made legal for people suffering from an incurable disease, with 36 percent opposed and 14 percent expressing no view on the subject. The results were surprising since 90 percent of Polish people are Catholics and both the Catholic Church and the Polish government are opposed to euthanasia.

▼ Janusz Switaj lies at home in his parents' apartment in Poland. Janusz requested euthanasia because he feels that he has no reason to continue living.

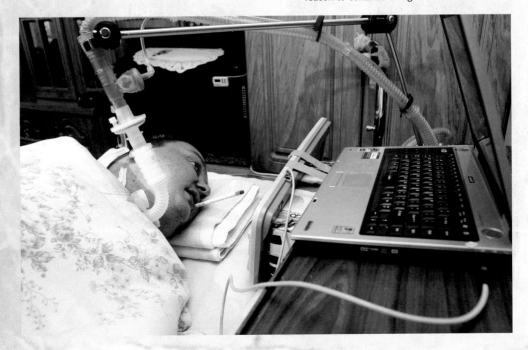

Debate About Euthanasia

In the twenty-first century, the debate on euthanasia has come to the forefront in many countries.

The media has played an important part in this debate. It has highlighted attempts to change the legal situation and the views of the medical profession. In the few countries that have legalized euthanasia, the media has analyzed how the law is being used or abused.

Above all, the media has featured the stories of people who request euthanasia for themselves or for family members. The stories have aroused both sympathy and revulsion, and often ignited passionate debate on the rights and wrongs of euthanasia and assisted suicide. In recent years, there have been media-led debates in countries as diverse as Australia, Canada, the Czech Republic, France, Ireland, Italy, Mexico, New Zealand, Poland, Spain, the United States, and the UK.

Yet euthanasia is an issue that directly affects only a small number of people. In countries where euthanasia is legal, only a few people request it and many do not actually go through with it.

In 2005, the Netherlands recorded 2,325 deaths from euthanasia, 100 cases of physician-assisted suicide, and 550 cases where the patient's life was ended without an explicit request from the patient. A total of 33,700 people also died from pain relief that probably hastened death and 21,300 after potentially life-saving treatment was abandoned. In Oregon in 2007, physicians wrote 85 prescriptions for lethal medication. Of these, 46 patients died from the medication, 26 died of their disease, and 13 were still alive at the end of the year. It seems that there will always be an unbridgeable gap between supporters and opponents of euthanasia. For supporters, it is a human right for patients in distress to choose how and when they want to die. Very often, people who make that choice

▼ Anti-euthanasia protesters demonstrate outside the Dutch parliament in April 2001 as parliamentarians prepare to vote to legalize euthanasia under certain conditions.

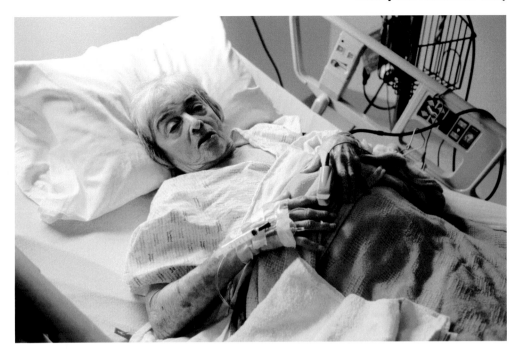

▲ Despite sickness and frailty, this women recovering from a hernia operation still believes her life has quality and meaning.

either die before their wishes can be put into effect or decide not to exercise their choice—it is the right to choose that is important rather than the act itself. Supporters regard euthanasia as an ethical option.

For opponents, euthanasia is a denial of the right to life. They say that the availability of good palliative care means that euthanasia should never be considered as an option. Furthermore, euthanasia goes against established medical ethics which say that doctors must act to preserve life, not take it away. Critics say that euthanasia is easily open to abuse and will target the most vulnerable people.

Despite the passionate arguments put forward on both sides, many people continue to feel unsure and uneasy about euthanasia. Perhaps the situation was best summed up by the report of the 2007 British Social Attitudes survey (see page 43), which said: "The public does not regard euthanasia in the black and white

terms in which it tends to be regarded by its advocates and opponents." It seems that the debate will continue for many years in the future.

summary

► There are organizations supporting or opposing euthanasia.

► The media has played an important part in the debate about euthanasia.

► Public opinions polls have shown a majority of people in favor of legalizing euthanasia under certain conditions, but few people see it as a black-and-white issue.

Glossary

Autonomy The ability for a person to do or decide something independently.

Debilitating Causing weakness or feebleness.

Degenerative When cells, tissues, and systems break down and function less and less effectively, making continued life difficult and painful.

Dementia An incurable disease in which a person loses his or her memory and personality—it mainly affects elderly people.

Dignity Having respect in your own eyes and the eyes of others.

Disability and/or disabled Problems with complete or proper functioning of parts of the body and or the mind.

Eugenics A once-popular "science" studying the improvement of the human race through selective breeding, now discredited.

Euthanasia The deliberate killing of a person, by themselves or others, for the benefit of that person.

Evaluate To measure or assess something.

Immunity In medical terms, the ability to resist or overcome infection. For example, if people have had a disease as a child, they may have immunity as an adult; vaccination also gives immunity.

Impunity Acting without punishment or consequences.

Indigenous people A tribal group who are the original inhabitants of a particular land, before other peoples settle there. For instance, the Inuit of Canada, Native Americans, and Aboriginal Australians.

Living will A document made by people to state the course of action they want if they become terminally ill or incapacitated, including wishes for when life-saving medical treatment should be used or withdrawn.

Manslaughter A death caused by one individual that is judged to be nonintentional or accidental; legally it is regarded as less serious than murder.

Medical ethics The principles that govern the way in which doctors and other medical professionals conduct their work and their relationship with their patients.

Minimally conscious state (MCS) A condition in which a person has brain damage but retains some consciousness and may eventually recover.

Mortality Death.

Palliative Something that can stop or lessen pain or other unpleasant symptoms without curing the condition.

Persistent vegetative state (PVS) A state whereby a person is conscious but brain dead and without autonomous body functions.

Principles Rules, standards, or guidelines for conduct.

Prosecute To bring legal proceedings against a person or company, usually in court.

Stimuli Things that animate the senses, used in medicine to see if someone can response to movement, light and sound, or pain.

Suicide Deliberate self-killing.

Terminal illness A disease or condition that will inevitably result in death, not necessarily quickly or immediately.

Timeline

1942 Article 115 of the penal code of Switzerland comes into effect, stating that assisting suicide is a crime only if the motive is selfish.

1980s Swiss clinics, run by organizations such as Dignitas, begin to offer assisted suicide to terminally ill people, including foreigners who come to Switzerland to die.

1994 The state of Oregon passes Death with Dignity Act, allowing euthanasia under certain conditions.

1995–6 A new law allows euthanasia in Australia's Northern Territory but is later repealed.

1999 Albania legalizes euthanasia for terminally ill people.

2001 The Netherlands passes a law stating that doctors will not be prosecuted for assisting terminally ill patients to die if they follow agreed procedures.

2002 Belgium legalizes euthanasia under certain conditions.

2007 Thailand legalizes a limited form of euthanasia.

2008 Luxembourg begins the process of legalizing euthanasia.

2010 A suspension of estate taxes for the year means that some terminally ill patients in the United States contemplate euthanasia so that their heirs will benefit.

Further Information and Web Sites

Books:

Euthanasia
by Carrie L Snyder (Greenhaven Press, 2006)

Euthanasia
by Linda Jackson (Heinemann-Raintree, 2005)

Euthanasia And The Right To Die
by Renee C Rebman (Enslow Publishers, 2002)

Web Sites

Due to the changing nature of Internet links, Rosen Publishing has developed an online list of Web Sites related to the subject of this book. This site is regularly updated. Please use this link to access this list:
http://www.rosenlinks.com/eth/euth

Index